THINGS TO DO NOW THAT YOU'RE 60

First published in Great Britain in 2005
by Spruce, an imprint of
Octopus Publishing Group Ltd
Carmelite House
50 Victoria Embankment
London EC4Y 0DZ
www.octopusbooks.co.uk

An Hachette UK Company
www.hachette.co.uk

The authorized representative in the
EEA is Hachette Ireland,
8 Castlecourt Centre,
Dublin 15, D15 XTP3, Ireland
(email: info@hbgi.ie)

This edition published in 2025
by Hamlyn

Distributed in the US by
Hachette Book Group
1290 Avenue of the Americas
4th and 5th Floors
New York, NY 10104

Distributed in Canada by
Canadian Manda Group
664 Annette St.
Toronto, Ontario, Canada M6S 2C8

ISBN 978-0-60063-875-9

A CIP catalogue record for this book is
available from the British Library.

Printed and bound in China

10 9 8 7 6 5 4 3 2 1

Publisher: Lucy Pessell
Designer: Dani Leigh & Isobel Platt
Senior Editor: Tim Leng
Assistant Editor: Samina Rahman
Production Manager: Peter Hunt

Picture Credits: iStock

MIX
Paper | Supporting
responsible forestry
FSC
www.fsc.org
FSC® C144853

THINGS TO DO NOW THAT YOU'RE 60

hamlyn

INTRODUCTION

Sixty year olds used to be old. They really did! Charles Dickens didn't even reach sixty, dying aged 58, but having worked so hard that he looked 80.

These days, 60-year-olds are often fitter and healthier-looking than their grown-up children. They can also look to Tom Cruise and Jennifer Connelly (who somehow both appear only a handful of years older than they did in the 1980s) as their elders. A person's sixties is a decade of ripeness and enjoyment, and of reaping rewards.

Being in your sixties today is far better than it used to be: from fitness, health, food and dietary awareness, to fashion, cosmetics and leisure activities. You can take on any projects (creative, personal or business) that you have always wanted to, help with charities to give something back or finally act selfishly for the first time in your life and do something that makes you feel truly special. All while staying fit and healthy and looking better than your grandparents did in their forties. Your sixties are a decade of exploration, accomplishment and personal growth: you have a lot left to give, and other lives still to live.

Because you are 60, your friends and family may start looking to you as a source of wisdom and experience. Preserve the illusion – nod sagely and say little.

You are different things to different people. Make a list of who you are at the moment – spouse, colleague, parent, child...Don't let one aspect dominate all the others.

Form a quiz team of friends with varying ages. You could offer to be the specialist on the 1970s...

Forget how old you are.

“Spring still makes spring in the mind, When 60 years are told: Love wakes anew this throbbing heart. And we are never old.”

RALPH WALDO EMERSON

Treat yourself and a friend to a night in a five-star hotel. Order the best champagne and caviar, live like a diva for an evening.

Go to a local court case with a friend or relative. Afterward, enjoy arguing with one another about the verdict.

If you ever wanted a tattoo when you were younger, but were always forbidden, now's the time to get one!

Never stop listening to your inner child. "A man at 16 will prove a child at 60."

18TH-CENTURY PROVERB

Decide which of your friends you can depend upon to give you an honest opinion. Stick pretty close to them when your ideas get too fanciful.

Plant a friendship garden. Find out the flower each of your friends loves most and give up a part of your garden to these plants.

RECORD A HUMOROUS MESSAGE ON YOUR ANSWERPHONE.

If you can, incorporate both love and friendships in your life. “Love is like the wild rose-briar, Friendship like the holly-tree – The holly is dark when the rose-briar blooms But which will bloom most constantly?”

EMILY BRONTË

Think about all of the positive things friends and relations have said about you to your face over the years. Try to live up to them.

Don't let the years slip by without having a really big celebration. Organize a big party and see how many family members from near and far you can get to attend.

Find a friend you can be happily silent with, and go for a long walk on a sunny afternoon together.

Never stop innovating and solving your own problems. In 1886, exasperated by the number of dishes broken in the kitchen by her family and servants, Mrs Josephine Cochrane of Illinois retired to the garden woodshed and invented the first dishwashing machine.

There are
only two ways to live your
life. One is as though nothing
is a miracle. The other is as
though everything
is a miracle.

ALBERT EINSTEIN

HOPE TO BE REMEMBERED. DO SOMETHING TO MAKE SURE THAT YOU ARE.

Be welcoming. Never forget you have the experience and confidence to deal with any situation.

There is nothing better that you can be than a friend in times of need. Show up when others are turning their backs.

Start trawling secondhand stores. You'll find them a source of imaginative and thoughtful (but inexpensive) gifts for friends and family.

Remember, you may still have dozens of responsibilities, but during the fantastic era of retirement, you owe it to yourself to be you.

TELL YOUR FRIENDS AND FAMILY THERE ARE NO LONGER ANY CURFEWS IN YOUR LIFE. YOU ARE GAME FOR ANYTHING AT ANY TIME.

The happiest part
of a man's life is what he
passes lying awake in
bed in the morning.

SAMUEL JOHNSON

Chill out, learn to break habits once in a while, and see what new opportunities present themselves. You can teach an old dog new tricks.

BUILD ON YOUR SUCCESSES, AND NEVER DWELL ON YOUR FAILURES.

LOOK AT ALL THE PEOPLE WHO HAVE REINVENTED THEMSELVES AFTER 60, AND LEARN SOME SMART IDEAS.

Make a list of the jobs (voluntary or paid) that you would like to try. Remember Maxim Gorky's adage, "When work is a pleasure, life is a joy. When work is a duty, life is slavery!"

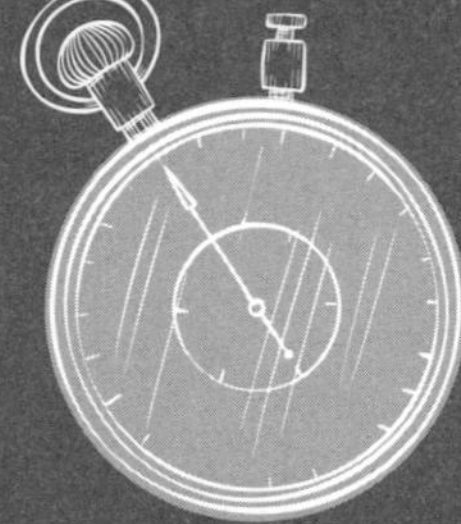

Tolerate each other's hobbies. John Harrison, a humble British watchmaker, spent most of his life trying to perfect a marine chronometer that would transform navigation at sea by determining longitude accurately. In the process, he turned his small house into a virtual workshop. His second wife put up with the chaos for decades. Harrison was over 60 before his chronometer finally worked: he was awarded a large cash prize by Parliament and changed the history of navigation.

Help to teach a child in your family how to read – or volunteer to read with children at a local school.

Make a list of organizations you admire, then pick one and take steps to become a member.

Go through your list of long-held likes and dislikes. Select one of your likes that is so way-out that you cannot believe that anyone else could share it with you. Then look for someone who does.

Make friends of as many different ages as possible. If you want to be, you can be the sage mentor to the young, and the giddy, irresponsible youth to those older than you.

Write a letter to your children telling them the single most important thing you have learned now you are 60.

Never get rid of your children's toys; your grandchildren will be fascinated by them and the fact that they used to belong their parents.

Make some decisions about what you really want out of life. "A lifestyle is what you pay for; a life is what pays you."

THOMAS LEONARD

SHARE YOUR HOBBIES AND INTERESTS. LOOK FOR GROUPS OF LIKE-MINDED PEOPLE.

There are many criteria for selecting new friends, but the best is still the good old-fashioned gut feeling. Trust your instincts.

When your children leave home, regard it as a gap year, not a permanent absence. They'll be back soon!

Believe in what you are doing. The playwright Tennessee Williams wrote some outstanding plays and a number of flops. He kept on writing because, as he said, “It means freedom of being, and if you can’t be yourself what’s the point of being anything at all?”

Get out and about.

"Without new experiences something inside of us sleeps."

FRANK HERBERT

If you want to go on a Caribbean cruise at Christmas instead of spending it with your adult children, don't feel guilty: just do it.

LEARN A NEW SKILL: PUTTING YOURSELF FIRST.

Continue to involve your children in your life. Take them into your confidence. Talk to them about how you want your life to change.

REMEMBER BEING A GRANDPARENT IS THE DELUXE VERSION OF PARENTHOOD. YOU GET TO HAVE A SPECIAL TIME WITH THE GRANDKIDS – AND THEN HAND THEM BACK!

Use your family tree as the basis for the writing of a family history. Gather anecdotes from relatives about grandparents, great-aunts, and great-uncles.

Regard your new life as a game of bridge – know when and what to discard.

BE GRATEFUL FOR WHAT YOU'VE HAD – AND STILL HAVE.

REFUSE TO BE TYPECAST. IT'S PERFECTLY POSSIBLE TO BE A HIGHLY SUCCESSFUL GRANDPARENT – AND BE SEXY WITH IT.

Prepare a timeline, with events from your family history above the line, and national and international events below it. Present your collection to the rest of your family. It's always a thrill to learn about family history.

Value and cherish the past, but don't be trapped by it. Always look forward to the future.

Nothing worth
knowing can be
understood with
the mind.

WOODY ALLEN

"A middle-aged person has likely learned to have a little fun in spite of his troubles."

DON MARQUIS

Look back over the last few years and decide which parts of your life have given you the most fulfilment. Devote more time to those over the next few years.

Don't lose your ambitions. It may be too late to start a fashion empire, but you could start making clothes for yourself and look into supplying garments for local boutiques.

Hunt around for all the leisure-time projects you have abandoned over the years. Now's your chance to pick up where you left off.

There's nothing more enjoyable than losing yourself in a hobby. Devote one day of every week to doing a creative hobby when you are not to be disturbed.

Rejuvenate yourself by dispensing with long-standing rituals.

Prepare for your new life of freedom and activity by doing some research: get acquainted with five hobbies you always fancied, and five you never thought of before.

We cannot live
only for ourselves.
A thousand fibers
connect us with our
fellow men; and
among those fibers, as
sympathetic threads,
our actions run as
causes, and they come
back to us as effects.

HERMAN MELVILLE

TURN THE COMPLAINT “I WISH I COULD” INTO THE MANTRA “I CAN.”

YOU’VE WORKED HARD FOR YEARS. NOW IT’S TIME TO PLAY HARD.

There’s always more to learn, no matter how much you think you know. Why don’t you start taking evening classes?

Visit Uluru National Park (formerly Ayers Rock) in Australia. This is a huge red rock growing out of a sandy plain in the Northern Territory. Uluru is an area of great cultural and religious significance to the aboriginal people and is a beautiful place to visit.

Get accustomed to the idea that your time is your own. Don't let anyone take it away from you.

A NEW LIFE IS WAITING FOR YOU. DON'T BE SURPRISED IF YOU FIND IT IN SOME UNUSUAL PLACES.

Borrow any written records – diaries and letters – left over from the older generations that relatives are prepared to let you have. Put them in secure folders and store them for generations to come.

The pessimist sees difficulty in every opportunity. The optimist sees the opportunity in every difficulty.

WINSTON CHURCHILL

NEVER STOP LEARNING – IT'S NOT SOMETHING YOU CAN COMPLETE.

Brush up on your jigsaw puzzle techniques. Always start by putting the four corner pieces in place, then assemble the sides. Only bend a piece out of shape as a last resort or at the height of frustration!

Don't throw your guitar and your musical ambitions away. Be daring and form a musical group. You've got more life experience to pour into musical expression now than when you were a kid.

ABRAHAM LINCOLN ONCE SAID, “EVERY MAN IS SAID TO HAVE HIS PECULIAR AMBITION.” PURSUE YOUR AMBITIONS EVEN IF THEY SEEM UNUSUAL TO OTHERS; THEY’RE YOURS.

Wallow in nostalgia. Visit a bar that you frequented as a youngster and check out how much it has changed.

Invent a new cocktail, made from ingredients of your choice. Give it a name that's in tune with your age and ambitions. Enjoy responsibly!

REDISCOVER THE JOYS OF THE AFTERNOON SNOOZE.

Treasure the knowledge that the older you get, the more memories you will have. “What greater thing is there for two human souls than to feel that they are joined...to strengthen one another.”

GEORGE ELIOT

In the lead-up to his sixtieth birthday, author Norman Mailer read over a hundred books on ancient Egypt while researching for his novel *Ancient Evenings*. Find a subject that fascinates you and research it thoroughly.

Watch old black and white movies with stars you've almost forgotten... in the afternoon, with the curtains drawn.

Start going to the cinema on your own – the emptier the screening, the better. After a lifetime of work, it is one of the most deliciously decadent pastimes.

Re-read a book you adored when you were young, and see how your reaction to it has changed. Ask someone you admire for their recommendation and read that too.

If you've always wanted to write a novel, this is the time to do it. Draw on your experiences and you'll be halfway there.

It is said that experience recollected in tranquillity can be a great spur. Make a collection of your most interesting memories.

Try your hand at writing poetry then submit your best example to one of the hundreds of poetry competitions in existence.

Love, all alike, no season
knows, nor clime, nor
hours, days, months, which
are the rags of time.

JOHN DONNE

Help improve your writing and at the same time get organized: start a diary.

Write poetry – but start small. The shortest poem in existence is said to be the anonymous: "Adam Had 'em." Can you find, or write, a shorter poem?

After a few weeks, assess your diary – look at the occasions that you enjoyed and those that you didn't. It's a good way of making the way you spend your time more positive and pleasurable to yourself.

Young love is a flame;
very pretty, often very
hot and fierce, but still
only light and flickering.
The love of the older
and disciplined heart is
as coals, deep burning,
unquenchable.

HENRY WARD BEECHER

CELEBRATE YOUR BIRTHDAY BY WALKING A MILE A DAY FOR EACH YEAR OF YOUR LIFE.

Start looking for games or sports that someone of 60 can win by years of carefully developed cunning, rather than by athletic ability!

On your travels, get off the beaten track. Be an explorer, not a tourist.

Consider a career change – you're never too old. Dwight D Eisenhower, the Allied Supreme Commander in World War II, had never shown any great interest in politics. Yet in the 1950s, he accepted the Republican nomination for President of the USA and (past his sixtieth birthday) won by a large majority; he was re-elected in 1956.

Take up debating, breadmaking, mah-jongg, chess, salsa, or high board diving – don't just stick to the tennis club.

Plant a tree to announce your sixtieth year. Grow with it.

Start a sketchbook. Make sketches of scenes that attract you. This is the perfect time of life to become an artist: you have experience, freedom, and wisdom on your side.

YOU CAN REACH THE TOP OF YOUR PROFESSION AFTER YOU'RE 60. THE EXPERIENCE AND INFORMATION YOU HAVE PICKED UP OVER THE YEARS ARE INVALUABLE.

Surprise yourself: learn about art history, music, ballet, theatre, or anything you've never had interest in before.

Some of our contact with others takes the form of nonverbal communication. Discover what your own posture and movement say about you.

Make a list of the people you've always got on best with. Why do you get on with them? Can you use this information to discover how to deal with other people you meet?

He who lives in
harmony with himself
lives in harmony
with the universe.

MARCUS AURELIUS

**Whatever you
can do or dream,
you can begin it.
Boldness has genius,
power, and magic
in it. Begin it now.**

**JOHANN WOLFGANG
VON GOETHE**

Owning a pet is deeply therapeutic and good for your emotional health.

Turn unwanted items into cash by selling them. Spend the proceeds on something unexpected.

Local amateur dramatic societies are always on the lookout for enthusiastic new members – even if just offering backstage skills such as carpentry or lighting, they should fall upon you with glee.

There are plenty of youth organizations that are desperate for leaders and helpers. Go and share your experience and get a whole new perspective on life.

You can search for treasure without a metal detector: the seashore, after the tide has gone out, is a good place for finds.

Eat out as much as possible and broaden your appreciation of exciting cuisines.

In 1894, humorist Mark Twain was almost 60 and contemplating bankruptcy. He was a poor businessman and had lost most of his money in the invention of a typesetting machine, which had failed. Twain refused to be dispirited. “Take heart,” he joked to his wife, “the worst is yet to come.” He was forced into bankruptcy but settled down, in his sixties, to a feverish regime of writing and within a few years had paid off all his creditors in full, although legally he was not forced to do so. “Honor,” he explained simply, “is a harder master than the law.”

GET A THOROUGH MEDICAL CHECK-UP EVERY SIX MONTHS, EVEN IF YOU THINK THERE IS NOTHING WRONG WITH YOU.

Note the three main components of fitness – flexibility, strength, and stamina. Look for enjoyable activities that will enhance your quota of each.

Take a fresh look at your lifestyle and assess where things need to change. Are you eating your five portions of fruit and vegetables a day?

Put any bad memories
firmly behind you.
"I sit beside my lonely fire,
And pray for wisdom yet:
for calmness to remember
or courage to forget."

CHARLES HAMILTON
AIDE

Take time to study everything you see. Look for its inner and outer beauty. The artist John Constable said, “I never saw an ugly thing in my life: for let the form of an object be what it may – light, shade, and perspective will always make it beautiful.”

Cut down on fatty foods and reduce your intake of salt and sugar to give your metabolism a head start.

Take heed of the old adage, "Breakfast like a king, lunch like a prince, and dine like a pauper." Make breakfast the most exciting meal of the day with some exotic fruits.

No excuses – start exercising right now! Research shows that people over 55 who exercise improve strength and fitness just as effectively as those in their twenties and thirties.

If you don't already have a green thumb, take up gardening and turn your backyard into that blooming haven of tranquillity you have always wanted it to be.

Go for a weekly walk with a friend. You'll get some gentle exercise, have a chance to catch up on the gossip, and occasionally it's good to have someone to help you home!

Time yourself over a one-mile walk. Repeat the walk every day and time yourself at monthly intervals to watch your progress.

Behind us as we go,
all things assume
pleasing forms, as
clouds do far off.

RALPH WALDO
EMERSON

Kill two birds with one stone: incorporate everyday activities such as gardening, maintenance and housework into your exercise plan.

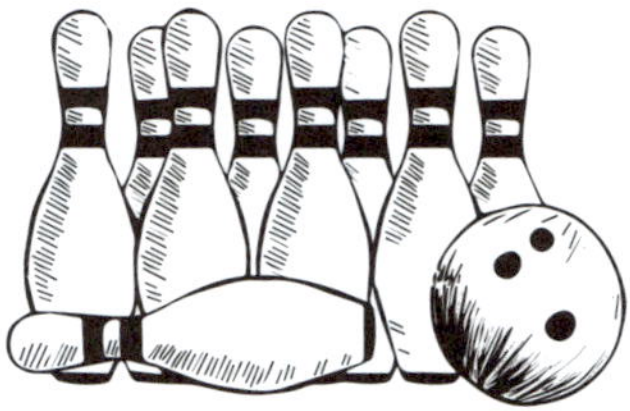

GO TEN-PIN BOWLING WITH YOUR GRANDCHILDREN. IT'S A GREAT SPORT FOR PEOPLE OF ALL AGES.

Go to at least two gigs a month, of some kind or other – even open mics at a local bar.

Become a local historian. John McNamara worked for the New York Housing Authority for almost 40 years, but he spent every spare moment investigating the streets of the Bronx. He used canoes and kayaks to cover all the waterways in the area. After his sixtieth birthday he published a definitive history of the Bronx called *History in Asphalt*.

Remember that it is a good thing to think deeply, but not to the exclusion of all else. As Oliver Edwards said, “I have tried too in my time to be a philosopher, but, I don’t know how, cheerfulness was always breaking in.”

Try yoga – it develops the body's physical, emotional, and spiritual aspects through movement, control of the will and emotions, and meditation.

Try a competitive sport. Getting a little competitive gets your adrenaline going and keeps the activity exciting and engaging.

To aid relaxation (especially after all your sporting efforts), enrol on a course of acupuncture.

**As human beings,
our greatness lies not
so much in being able
to remake the world...
as in being able to
remake ourselves.**

MAHATMA GANDHI

Throw away any preconceived notions about chronological age. In retirement, you'll have the joy of being an absolute beginner at new things.

Explore this formula for achieving inner peace and satisfaction as you grow older: seek to have something to do, something to strive for, and someone to love.

IF YOU'VE TAKEN ON TOO MUCH, TAKE A STEP BACK EVERY NOW AND AGAIN. DON'T ALLOW YOURSELF TO FEEL TRAPPED IN YOUR LIFE.

BE PROUD OF YOUR MATURITY, DON'T DENY IT.

Use your experience to seek equilibrium in your life at this important stage. Think, feel, believe and act.

Enjoy each moment. Your experience will have told you by now that good things do not always last, so make the most of each enjoyable event until the next one comes along, as it surely will.

Wheresoever
you go, go with
all your heart.

CONFUCIUS

Don’t let age deter you from going anywhere. The Danish explorer Vitus Bering was 60 when he embarked upon his last great voyage.

Retirement is essentially your time. Get used to being good to yourself and putting yourself first for a change.

REFUSE TO CONFORM TO STEREOTYPES OF AGE. YOU ARE YOU.

Work at self-improvement, whether you're tackling trivial things or bigger soul-searching issues.

Look to the future. We have all accumulated baggage. The trick is not to keep unpacking it.

Don't avoid problems. Every time you successfully solve one, it will increase your confidence and self-esteem.

Plan to make your next year a voyage of self-discovery. Embark upon your journey with enthusiasm. Be prepared to be flexible – mentally as well as physically.

Look after yourself, but enjoy yourself in the process. “The best doctors in the world are Dr Diet, Dr Quiet, and Dr Merryman.”

JONATHAN SWIFT

Have some of your reactions to situations become too automatic? Try to take each new situation as it comes. Reflect upon your alternatives before deciding on a course of action.

Remember to laugh when things go wrong. Then you will always have a smile on your face, no matter what life throws at you.

Remember to look back and appreciate what you have done in your life. Don't waste time regretting what you haven't done.

Look to your health
and if you have it,
praise God, and value it
next to a good conscience.

IZAAC WALTON

Plan to sit in your garden and enjoy it as often as you work in it. "Nothing so pleasant as to sit amid that mixture of flower and leaf, watching the bee-bird. Nothing so pretty as my garden."

MARY RUSSELL MITFORD

Decide which attributes you have developed over the years. How are you different to when you were 20, and how can you take advantage of that?

Smile. It reduces stress. The physical act prompts the mind to release chemicals that trigger pleasant emotions.

MOTIVATE YOURSELF BY PROMISING YOURSELF A TREAT AFTER ANY GRUELLING ACHIEVEMENT OR CHORE.

Take the time to encourage others. It will make you feel good about yourself and people will appreciate your consideration.

Be specific in your intentions. Break challenges down into their smallest possible components and the task will become far less daunting.

COMMUNICATE. WHEN YOU UNDERSTAND YOURSELF, SEEK TO BE UNDERSTOOD BY OTHERS.

Take heart – you've still got sex appeal. Actor Sean Connery was 60 years old when he was nominated by *Playboy* magazine as the world's sexiest man. "It'll be all downhill from here," he sighed.

TUNE IN TO YOUR EMOTIONS, BUT DON'T BE GOVERNED BY THEM.

Remember that you must make the final choices about your life yourself. Don't rely on your partner or friends to push you in a particular direction – even though they might have your best interests at heart.

Revisit your spiritual side. If you've never given much thought to God or any Supreme Being, decide what place a supreme being has in your life.

Some books seem to have been
written not to teach us anything,
but to let us know that the
author has known something.

JOHANN WOLFGANG
VON GOETHE

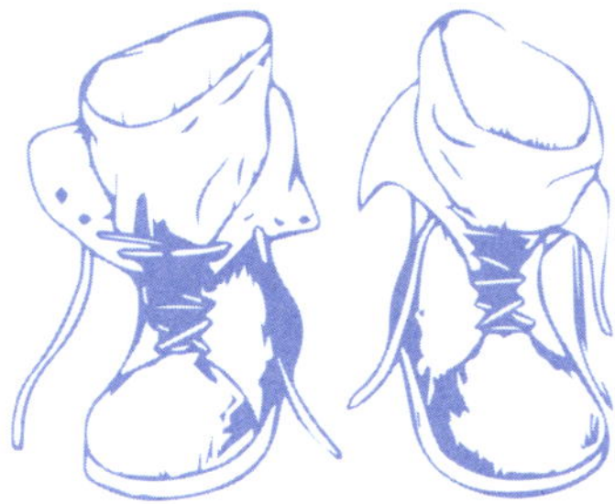

A walk is one of the secrets
for dodging old age.

RALPH WALDO EMERSON

Remain in contact with others. No matter how engrossing your hobby or work, social interaction with others is an essential factor in maintaining mental and physical alertness.

Well in advance of retirement, sort out your financial situation. Get forecasts of pensions and annuities. Study interest rates on savings.

Write down your daily expenses and see if you can cut back on unnecessary spending. Put aside what you save in a savings account and get yourself an expensive luxury in a year's time.

Strive to do many things, but be sure to concentrate and remain focused on only one thing at a time to get the most from it.

Two great aids to retaining mental agility are generally held to be creativity and concentration. Try to use them in combination – for example in painting, a hobby that can be taken up at any age.

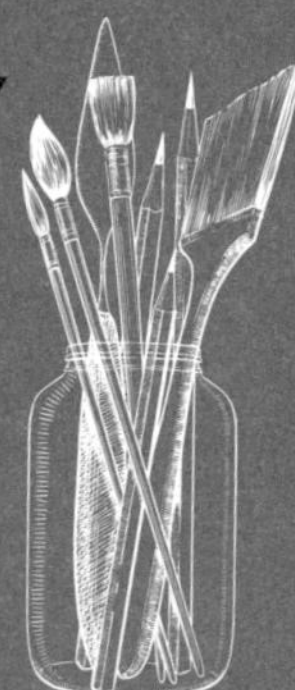

MAKE PLANS TO READ ALL THE BOOKS YOU HAVE ALWAYS WANTED TO READ.

Better hunt in fields for health unbought, Than fee the doctor for a nauseous draught, The wise, for cure, on exercise depend; God never made his work for man to mend.

JOHN DRYDEN

Don't forget you still have a lot to offer, as employee or volunteer. Strong points of older workers are stability, reliability, commitment, responsibility, and maturity.

CONSIDER DEVELOPING A HOBBY INTO A SECOND CAREER.

Look at advertisements for voluntary workers in sectors you never worked in before – you might discover a new talent, or passion.

Make the most of your family connections as you grow older. LaVell Edwards, football coach at Brigham Young University, was one of 14 children. He said that the university did not dare fire him, because his family bought so many tickets for each game!

Let those who would
write heroic poems
make their life an
heroic poem.

JOHN MILTON

Don’t dress how you think someone your age ought to – after all, thanks to exercise and diet, many 60-year-olds are in better shape than their grown-up children.

Take advice, but don’t let it interfere with your plans. You are old enough to know your own mind by now.

BE ENTHUSIASTIC. IF YOU’RE GOING TO DO WHAT YOU WANT TO DO, DO IT WITH GUSTO AND ENJOYMENT.

DO EVERYTHING YOU DO WITH STYLE.

If your children are leaving home, let go and be proud of them. They are entitled to a life too.

Always learn from your experiences, no matter how bad they may have seemed at the time.

Remember that friends and relations have been and will remain the sheet anchors in your life. Try to be the same for them.

Give something back to the environment after all these years of using its resources: devote the next few years to building a home that is eco-friendly, and incorporate natural materials.